You Are the Common Denominator in Your Life

"20 concepts that can change your life"

Success Handbook Series

Copyright © 2020 Revised Edition
by John Calabrese
"Published by SkillBites, www.skillbites.net"

All rights reserved. The right to reproduce this work in any form whatsoever is strictly prohibited without permission in writing from John Calabrese, except for brief passages in connection with a review

ISBN 978-1-952281-28-0

Contact us at

www.Growthisadecision.com

John@growthisadecision.com

Thank You

Thank you Grand Master Tom McGee, Grand Master Frank Cullerton, Kevin Trudeau, Esther Hicks, Ron Ball, Ed Foreman, Mary Miller and Troy McClain.

I want to thank all the great teachers that have taught and influenced me over the years.

Part One

Acknowledgements

Introduction

Chapter One: Live Outside the Box

Chapter Two: Work with the Universe not Against It

Chapter Three: The Power of Your Thoughts

Chapter Four: The Power of Your Words

Chapter Five: Personal Responsibility

Chapter Six: Persistence

Chapter Seven: Aim High

Chapter Eight: Invest in Yourself

Chapter Nine: Mindfulness

Chapter Ten: Take Care of Your Health

In Summary

Part Two

Introduction

Chapter One: Gratitude

Chapter Two: Beliefs

Chapter Three: Feeling Good

Chapter Four: Decisions

Chapter Five: Choices

Chapter Six: Either a Gift or a Lesson

Chapter Seven: Who and What Do You Surround Yourself With?

Chapter Eight: Live the Life You Want to Live

Chapter Nine: Work on Yourself

Chapter: Ten: Be a Good Friend to Yourself

Final Words

You Are The Common Denominator In Your Life!

10 Concepts That Can Change Your Life!

We are going to explore ten concepts that, if applied, can improve your life. At the end of each chapter take a few minutes to contemplate the concept, then evaluate where you are currently in relation to it.

You are the Common Denominator in Your Life. What that means is that you are at the center of everything. Everything you think, want and do creates your life. You affect every area of your life. How about your relationships? The key is you. Let's not forget your job or profession. No one else can step into your shoes and make those daily career decisions but you. Your health is mostly determined by the choices you make. Only you can make the decisions and initiate every action in your life. Ultimately, you are the person who is affected by the outcomes of your decisions.

Many factors determine who you are. Your life plays out according to your choices. A better you leads to a better life.

Being raised in poverty can influence your ability to achieve massive success, while a person from a wealthy family, who went to Harvard, seems to have the upper hand. These factors affect your accomplishments in life but can also be motivating forces. What contributes to the shaping of "you" is what you have been taught, personal experiences, beliefs, dreams, and your mental & physical health to name a few things.

From all of this you become who you are. When I say *who you are,* I am referring to your habits, beliefs and the attitudes you operate from. It isn't who you were at birth; it is who you become due to outside influences. Who you *truly* are is a conversation for another day.

Sometimes we are fortunate to have parents, relatives and teachers who give us great information, experiences and beliefs that help us to create wonderful lives. This does not mean those blessed with advantages will succeed. It means they have an advantage, but it is up to them to utilize it properly.
There are others of us who are not so fortunate. The information and beliefs given to us are limiting or worse yet, detrimental to our success in life.
Imagine the child born into poverty being led to believe that they can't get an education. They believe that they cannot break the chains of poverty

or achieve their dreams even though so many people have risen out of abject poverty and become outrageous successes. It comes down to what they have been taught and what they believe. We all have the right to reject things we were taught if they are not beneficial to us.

Many privileged people lead miserable and unfulfilled lives. On the other hand, a hard life can develop in a person, traits of indomitability, belief in themselves and a work ethic that allows them to climb to great heights.

Something as simple as a person's stress level can affect every area of their life. If someone is stressed to their limit, their communication, relationships and career will all be negatively impacted. They snap at their wife or coworker, causing strained relationships. They make errors at work. They are the common denominator in every area of their life. If they took the time and made the effort to address their stress levels, everything would improve.

Improve yourself and your life improves. The power and control rests within you.

We are going to explore ten concepts that can help you to take control over the shaping of your life. If applied, these concepts can turn you into a creator as opposed to a spectator of your life.

After each chapter there will be a page for you to write down some notes if you like. You can write what you gained from it, action steps you plan to take or points you would like to reflect on. I know by doing this you will benefit greatly. However, doing this is your choice.

Chapter One: Live Outside the Box

I want you to imagine for a moment that you have traveled 100-200 years into the past knowing what you know now. What would happen to you if you knew then what you know is possible now? Your understanding would be much greater than anyone else's. Would they understand, and expand their thinking? Or would you be locked up, ostracized or called crazy?

Many years ago, a man named Marconi had an idea that information could be transported through the air without wires and received at a distant location. He shared his ideas with his friends and instead of encouraging him they admitted him into a psych ward. When he got out, he invented a way to generate, transmit and receive radio waves.

When it was discovered that the earth revolves around the sun and not the other way around, the idea was met with incredible resistance. That idea led to the imprisonment of a man who thought outside the box named Galileo.

As much as we want to believe things are different today, not a lot has truly changed. Naturally, it is hard for people to venture outside of what is considered the norm. They may not give you poison to drink like they gave Socrates but being discredited and labeled crazy can be very devastating.

Albert Einstein once said, "The one who follows the crowd will usually get no further than the crowd. The one who walks alone, is likely to find himself in places no one has ever been"

People who stay in the box most likely will remain average. Those that dare to go outside the box open up more opportunities for greater success. They have removed the limitations that bind most people.

Oftentimes, the fear of criticism or the label of being a nut stifles the expansion of thought and creativity. In many cases, the level of creativity that someone allows themselves to have is governed by what people can handle. Imagine for a moment if all the great minds of the past were not persecuted or killed but were encouraged to expand to their full ability. What strides would have been made to the benefit of mankind?

You need to not care what others think. Pursue your dreams with everything you have. Be creative, think thoughts that no one has ever had and pursue them until they are a reality. Everything that has been created has at one point been a thought in someone's mind. Divergent thinking (outside the box) is the key.

Live the life you want to live regardless of what everyone else is doing. Somehow there was a life's script given to everyone to follow: Go to college, get a job, get married, have children, buy a house with a white picket fence with a dog then work 9:00am -5:00pm, retire and die. Why limit yourself that way? Follow the path in life that is fulfilling and brings you happiness.

There is a saying in business "When everyone is buying, sell, when everyone is selling, buy." The point of that saying is that the greatest achievements come from the place where everyone isn't.

Outside the box is where all the amazing things are discovered. Why is this type of thinking so frowned upon? Sir Kenneth Robinson from England stated some very interesting information. He found in his research as an educational theorist that children age four through six are geniuses of divergent thinking (outside the box). They have no limits and believe they can do anything. Between the ages of six to eight they lose 60% of their ability to think that way. It gets worse between the ages of eight to ten as they lose another 20%. After the age of twelve they lose most of what is left. They conform to the mold society has imposed upon them.

If you want to discover or do something great, you must be willing to leave the box of normal thinking and strive for something amazing. Lose your fear of criticism and return to divergent thinking. Free yourself of the limits most people accept.

Remember, You are the Common Denominator in Your Life.

Notes

What did you learn?

What action steps can you take?

What points do you need to reflect on?

Chapter 2: Work with the Universe not Against it

There are many universal laws that you must adhere to such as the law of gravity, the law of lift, Emerson's law of compensation and the Universe's most senior law, the law of attraction. If you ignore these laws, you do so at your own peril.

I am mainly going to address the law of attraction.

The law of attraction is the universe's law and quantum physics is a study of it. It is the universe's supreme law. This law governs everything. It states that you have attracted and created everything in your life by your thoughts and subsequent actions. All actions start as a thought.

Quantum physics studies the atom and energy and tries to explain all of this through a scientific view.

To understand how this works there will be some things you will need to know. Some concepts you need to consider are; everything is energy, thoughts are things and the law of attraction is law.

Atoms are made of subatomic particles, which are not made of energy but are energy. You are made of atoms. I guess it is safe to say you and everything else are energy. Everything is following the way energy works and nothing is solid or static.
Everything is energy that is vibrating at different frequencies. Love vibrates differently than hate

does, metal vibrates differently than wood and so on.

The brain transmits energy or frequencies through your thoughts. It also receives a matching frequency back that comes to you in the form of your reality. A good example of how frequency works is if you are thinking and feeling thankfulness, the universe will return to you something to be thankful for. The frequencies are created by your thoughts and emotions. This works with both positive and negative frequencies. The more emotional intensity that one emits, the stronger the broadcast they put out. If you transmit a frequency of fear, you will receive back circumstances that match your fear.

Quantum physics is based on quantum mechanics, which states that atoms are only tendencies. In other words, nothing is set in how or where it is until you put mental thought on it. There may be several possible outcomes to a situation but the one your thoughts match is the one that is most likely to happen. Everything starts with multiple possibilities until they are observed and then they all collapse into the one. All things exist and are determined by your thoughts and attention to them. You are living in a sea of energy and everything is connected.

Earl Nightingale put it this way: "You become (or get) what you think about most of the time." You basically get or become the result of your predominant thoughts. It does not matter if they are positive or negative, or if you are thinking about what you want or what you don't want. All that is recognized is what you are thinking about.

One thing that is critical to know is that this all happens whether you consciously participate or not. The vast majority of people either don't even know this is how it works or lack the mental discipline to affect it in a deliberate, positive way.

Ignorance of this law basically puts you in a boat without a rudder with no one actively directing the outcome.

You may think this sounds simple: I will just think I want one million dollars and I will get it. Well, if you are putting out a matching frequency for what you want that would be true. It is important that you understand that the law of attraction does not necessarily hand you the specific thing you are wanting. It creates the opportunity, but you must take the action to make it happen. Here comes the bad news. There is a little more to it than that and there are subtleties that make it work. Are you wishing for a million dollars or do you believe you will have a million dollars? The law of attraction responds to beliefs, not wishes. Now what if you have in your core belief system that you could not have a million dollars, rich people are evil or making a million dollars is impossible? Your desire for a million dollars would be nullified by your core beliefs. The good news is that it is possible to reprogram your brain to think and broadcast differently. This means that you can deliberately set up what kind of thoughts you think and instruct your beliefs to line up with what you really want. You will need to replace your negative thought patterns with positive thought patterns.

Unfortunately, that is a little harder than it sounds. You are constantly surrounded by negative influences that corrupt your thinking. That is why you need to find surroundings that are positive. Everything from the people you are with to the information coming at you to your activities and so much more must be positive. Later in this book we will be discussing how martial arts can help with this as well as how to develop the skills to be able to use the law of attraction to your advantage.

Thought patterns are key. When you repeat a thought over and over it creates a neural pathway in your brain. Thoughts mixed with emotion emit a frequency. With time and repetition, they become stronger and emit that frequency automatically. Good thought patterns bring you success and bad thoughts bring negative outcomes.

There are many aspects to how this works, from quantum physics to the metaphysical. If you are new to this kind of information you may be on overload at this point.

Let me give you some examples of how this works. Have you ever really wanted something although it looks impossible and then you get it in an almost magical way? Or you think about someone you haven't seen in a long time and they call you out of the blue. These are examples of energy in action.

Energy of thought is working all the time. You are always thinking and broadcasting thoughts. A great example of this would be if you're driving a car, the car is energy in motion. If you have a blindfold on and you're still driving, you have no awareness or control of where you are going. If you take off the blindfold you are fully engaged in the driving process. You are now in control and deliberately directing where you are going. Either way, the car is still moving and going somewhere.

This is a critical concept to grasp. The law of attraction is the way the Universe keeps everything happening in harmony. It is the law that, if understood and applied, allows you to create any life you want.

Picture a large matrix with every living thing entering its thoughts, hopes, dreams and actions into it. Picture this as a big jig saw puzzle, a matrix with unfathomable power to align everything that happens based on the frequencies we all emit. All these frequencies are weaved into a symphony called life.

We will touch on this concept throughout the remainder of the book.

Notes

What did you learn?

What action steps can you take?

What points do you need to reflect on?

Chapter Three: The Power of Your Thoughts

Your thoughts are things. It was discovered that your brain emits and receives energy or frequencies. This is how your reality is created. If this is hard to grasp check the writings of Albert Einstein, Nikola Tesla and Thomas Edison. A little-known fact is that Henry Ford, who was a master of using his mind to create went to great lengths to keep this information quiet for fear his workers would learn how to use it. He knew if they did, he could lose his work force.

The real key is to keep your thoughts more positive than negative. Whatever your predominant thoughts are, *mixed with emotion,* will most likely happen. If you are fearful or worried something bad is going to happen, it is very likely that it will happen. If you are focused on a promotion at work with anticipation of it happening, there is a good chance it will. However, the Universe is very unapologetic in how it delivers. You want a promotion and the next day you get fired, which leads to a new job with even more pay and benefits. The Universe does not hear the words or details just the emotion of it. It will match the emotions of what you want to what you get. For better or worse, the Universe has a tendency to over-deliver in both directions.

Buddha said, "You are the sum total of all your thoughts until today." Changing your thinking today changes your life going forward. Your current situation is the result of your thoughts in the past.

Change your thoughts today and create the future you want.

You can't control every thought you have nor do you need to. The important thing is to monitor the predominant thoughts you think with great repetition. These form neural pathways in the brain and as they grow, they have a bigger effect. A way to picture a neural pathway is see it as a groove in a record. Your thoughts affect your feelings. Thinking about a sad event makes you feel sad. It works both ways; your words will reflect your thinking and emotions. You can use your words to change your thoughts and emotions.

We will explore this concept more in Chapter 4.

There is a cycle that can form from your thinking. You think a thought about something you don't want over and over until it happens in your life. Now you focus and think about it even more strongly since you have to deal with it. This will bring about something even worse and this sequence continues to repeat itself. It is hard to break this loop or cycle. You must change your thought patterns and focus on what you do want. In the midst of your negative circumstances it is difficult to be in a positive mindset. That is why you can get trapped in this cycle.

The good news is this cycle is the same when you focus on things you do want. It creates momentum in a positive direction and your life gets better and better.

It really comes down to this. What are your predominant thoughts? Have you developed positive or negative thought patterns? What thoughts are you programming into your brain?

Notes

What did you learn?

What action steps can you take?

What points do you need to reflect on?

Chapter Four: The Power of Your Words

The words you use do have a frequency, which effects what you draw into your life. An important point to consider is your words help broadcast your emotions which are radiated from your brain as a frequency such as a high frequency of joy or a low frequency of hate. If you say with enthusiasm, "This is great," you can expect something great to happen because that is the emotion that will be matched. If you say with great emotion "This sucks" it isn't hard to see what you will be getting.

Choosing your words can have a big effect on what comes your way. Being careful with your words can also help you control your thoughts. Thinking and speaking work together. Control one and you affect the other. Your words and thoughts work in tandem.

Suppose you say, "I don't want to be late," and the Universe conspires to make you late. Do you ever wonder why that happens? It is because you stated energetically, through your thought frequency that you wanted to be late and the law of attraction helped you attract what you wanted; TO BE LATE. The Universe is all-inclusive. In other words, you only add what you want; you can't subtract what you don't want but you can replace it. Words like no, not, don't or any other similar words aren't recognized by our brain. What is even more profound is that they aren't even recognized by the Universe. If you say, "I don't want to be late," you get extra traffic to make you late. If you say, "I want to be on time," you seem to magically get all the green lights and extraordinarily light traffic. It is all in the thinking.

This concept is written in the Bible in phrases such as: "Ask and you shall receive," "Knock and the door shall be opened to you," and so many others. This is not a new age concept; it is as old as mankind.

You can use your words in a very deliberate way, stating often what you want with the knowing that you are just placing an order. Remember, the Universe does not judge what you say, it just delivers you a vibrational match to what you are feeling.

Lao Tzu, the author of the Tao Te Ching said:

"Be careful of your thoughts because they become your words.
Your words become your actions.
Your actions become your habits.
Your habits become your character and your character becomes your destiny"

Be careful of the words you use to program your brain. You program yourself to win or to lose. This also follows the concept that if you say or hear lies enough times you start to believe them. So, talk about what you want in your life. Thinking and talking about what you want will help you to believe you can have it.

Henry Ford puts it this way: "Whether you think you can, or you think you can't either way you are right. It is the thinking that makes it so." Remember, he was a master of using his mind to get what he wanted. Don't create self-imposed limitations by telling yourself and others you can't do something.

Sometimes it is better to keep your intentions to yourself because others may tell you that they think your goal is impossible. Their doubt may influence you to doubt you can do it. Doubt is fatal to your dreams.

Notes

What did you learn?

What action steps can you take?

What points do you need to reflect on?

Chapter Five: Personal Responsibility

A key thing to understand is that life and the Universe are governed by laws. We have the choice of adhering to or resisting them. Trying to defy the law of attraction is just as useless as resisting the law of gravity.

Know that your thoughts, words and beliefs control what happens in your life. Yes, you are in control of what happens in your life. Use these tools wisely and mindfully and create whatever you truly desire.

So many people live in a victim mentality. They want to blame other people and the circumstances they feel are being thrust upon them, when in reality they have created everything in their lives. Many people do this whether they acknowledge it or not. If you focus on what you want, that is what you will get. If you focus on what you don't want, you will get that too. You need to examine what you are predominately thinking about and focused on.

When you accept that you are responsible for everything that happens in your life you are liberated. You assume total control of your life. You may at times not understand how you did it, but with greater understanding of the law of attraction the insight will come to you. This is difficult for many people to accept.

Have you ever had a situation happen in your life and you didn't make a change? Then, you got a similar situation that was a bit more intense. This pattern is likely to continue until you learn the lesson and make a change. This is the Universe teaching you.

This can be a relationship that keeps repeating itself until you make a change in yourself. You have momentum on the subject.

What is Momentum?

Momentum is energy on a subject. It is a flow that can carry you.

Have you ever watched a sporting event when a team has a series of great plays and the commentator says this team has the momentum?

Momentum can be good or bad.

You can have momentum in your thinking, habits, dominant thoughts, actions, relationships, feelings, interests, thought patterns, and many other subjects.

An example of momentum is: You start a plan to exercise every day and you do until momentum carries it and forms a habit.

Momentum in a relationship could be that you are attracted to the same type of person and you continue to go into relationships with them. It doesn't mean that they are good for you. It means you do it on autopilot and because you have such strong momentum, the Universe puts the law of attraction into effect drawing the person into your life.

Let's say there is something that is upsetting to you and you think about it a lot with strong negative emotions. Every time this thought enters your mind you get upset. This causes you to think about it more and feel even stronger which, because of momentum, brings even more of it.

You may have an interest in something that leads to a magnificent obsession and outrageous success. For example, you could aspire to become an NFL quarterback or an international jewel thief. Remember, momentum doesn't recognize good or bad. There is no judgment, although going to the dark side does have ramifications beyond what the police will do. There is a difference between negative and positive energy and where they will take you.

Let's say you are in sales and you close a big deal. Then you make another sale and another. With the confidence and belief in yourself you gained from your successes; you gain momentum. In this example, you would be experiencing positive momentum and continue to make sales. You would have the feeling that this would continue.

Look at your habits. Do they have momentum? This, like all the examples can be a good thing or a bad thing. Energy does not make a judgment.

Your day is comprised of routines or habits. These days make up your months, years and your life.

Are your habits good or bad?

The real question is: Have your habits led you to the type of life you want? You can evaluate your habits, pick one that is the least helpful and change it. Then continue the process of eliminating bad habits until you are living the life you want. It can be said that you are the sum total of your habits.

There are three possible directions momentum can take you.

The first is a downward spiral. Any alcoholic can tell you about a downward spiral. This is when you experience a series of negative events and they make you feel like you are spinning out of control. You find yourself in a negative momentum cycle.

The second is the one in which momentum keeps you on a path to nowhere. You don't fail or succeed; you just stay in the same patterns, which are taking you nowhere.

The third is the upward spiral. You are succeeding and each success leads you to the next. This continues to add momentum with each new experience.

You will enter into momentum from one or more of the following three ways.

First, it is possible to consciously build momentum. You will knowingly try to start the flow. This can be done by going for smaller goals to get the process in motion. You may put several positive events close together to increase the effect of them. No matter how you do it the fact is that you are doing it deliberately.

Secondly, you are doing this subconsciously. You may have some residual momentum from your past that you activate through your thoughts and deeds. When you learn and develop a physical skill it gets to a point where you can do it with little to no effort. That is because you have developed neural pathways in your brain that fire through the nervous system making it automatic. You develop your thinking and thought patterns. Thought patterns can be developed to create either success or failure. What most people don't know is that you can choose what type of neural pathways you want to create. You literally program your subconscious mind with the thoughts and information you feed into it.

Thirdly, you are oblivious to the fact that you are starting and maintaining negative momentum on a subject. You may start thinking the same thoughts over and over, which will bring people, circumstances and events into your life that will feed that thinking. Now you are on a runaway train.

How do you stop momentum you don't want?

It is possible to identify that you have momentum on something you don't want. You make a decision and consciously break the momentum using your will and mindfulness. There will be times when you will identify the cycle you are in and not be strong enough to bring the momentum to a stop. Smoking, abusing alcohol and staying in bad relationships are all good examples of knowing something is bad but being unable to break free of it.

The most common method of breaking the grip of momentum is usually made through the assistance of the Universe, God or however you want to view it. You may crash and hit bottom or a major change in your life is thrust upon you. This may even appear to be a disaster, but it is a gift. A person may have momentum on the habit of not taking care of their health. They have all the bad habits and their health is steadily succumbing to the effects. Then they get a wake-up call such as someone close to them getting cancer or they have a heart attack. They get a jolt to their system and they have an opportunity to break free. The more extreme the situations causing this jolt are to their system the better.

Momentum can bring failure or success. You may be a victim of it or use it consciously to succeed. The decision is yours to make.

Now you have a choice to make. You can embrace taking responsibility for everything in your life or not. This is not an all or nothing choice. Start where you are. You can start slowly and accept what you can. The goal is to grow until you take full responsibility for everything in your life.

Notes

What did you learn?

What action steps can you take?

What points do you need to reflect on?

Chapter Six: Persistence

Persistence is an extremely valuable trait to have within you. Being persistent is often what makes the difference between success and failure.

Looking at the lives of many successful people and seeing the challenges they had to overcome on the way to success tells you everything you need to know about the importance of persistence.

Michael Jordan was cut from his high school basketball team. He did not give up. Instead, he gave his all and never quit. He exemplified the saying *quitters never win and winners never quit*. Growing up in Chicago and watching him play for the Chicago Bulls I am glad he didn't.

Babe Ruth is known for hitting a lot of home runs. He also set the record for the most strikeouts. Is he remembered for his home runs or his strikeouts? He understood two key things. First, is the law of averages; the more times he tried the more chances he had for success. Second was the difference between a temporary defeat and failure. Just a side note; do you know who broke his strikeout record? It was Mickey Mantle of the New York Yankees. That is called failing forward.

Look at Abraham Lincoln's life. He lost eight elections, experienced the death of his girlfriend and had a nervous breakdown on his way to becoming the President of the United States. Thinking about this I came to a question. Were all those challenges

39

a gift to him? Did they groom and temper him, prepare him for what he needed to be to be able to handle the tremendous task he undertook as a president in those times? Did the Universe align everything for his destiny, or did he create it? Or was it a co-creation?

Great success doesn't always come easily but when you are passionate about getting what you want you do whatever it takes. This can mean many temporary failures until you obtain what you want.

An investor friend of mine told me an interesting story. He was asking a very wealthy and successful investor to get involved in a project he was doing. He explained the project and asked her if she had any questions or wanted any additional information. She said, "I want you to tell me your nightmares, the deals that went horribly wrong". He was a little surprised and didn't see where this was going to be helpful to him and asked her why. She said "I don't do business with people who haven't failed big and overcome it. This is my litmus test". She knew very well people who stop after a failure never succeed. People who fail and keep going do succeed and that's whom she does business with.

I was at an event where I heard Donald Trump tell some very interesting stories of his temporary failures and how he overcame them.

He was walking out of a restaurant with his wife and said "You see that homeless man over there selling pencils? He is worth millions of dollars more than me right now." At the time he was millions of dollars in debt and was on the verge of losing everything. We all know he made it but the story I am about to share tells how he used the law of attraction to do it.

Donald Trump said something that was very interesting. He said, "Successful people do the things they don't want to do but know they should"

Mr. Trump then proceeded to tell a story that showed this concept and the law of attraction working in complete harmony.

This is not a direct quote, but I will paraphrase the best I can. Donald Trump was in his office when his assistant informed him that he had a black-tie event scheduled that evening. Not only that but it was with the bankers he was restructuring his debt with. Nine of the ten bankers were cooperating and working with him. One banker did not like him and was not being very cooperative. He needed all ten banks on board. It would only work if all ten banks agreed to cooperate. He went home and realized he needed to go, and he did. First, let me say there is no such thing as a coincidence. Guess who he was seated next to at the dinner? Yes, it was the tenth banker. It started out cold and awkward, but over the course of the evening the banker warmed up to him and became friendly. He said to come to his office, and he was sure they could work this all out. That is how the law of attraction works and how Donald Trump escaped a potentially disastrous situation.

He did not just wish or hope for a good outcome, he acted and the Universe lined things up for him. You must take continuous inspired action toward your goals and dreams.

Even using the law of attraction, lasting success does not happen overnight and can require persistent effort for its achievement.

Notes

What did you learn?

What action steps can you take?

What points do you need to reflect on?

Chapter Seven: Aim High

There is a wonderful quote, which is "Shoot for the moon. Even if you miss you are still up among the stars."

I teach in martial arts to aim through the target not at it. The bigger you think the bigger you will achieve.

That is not saying there are not smaller and intermediate goals that need to be achieved in route to the ultimate goal. You must keep your objective in mind but take all the steps necessary to achieve it.

You cannot hit a target you don't have. You need to have big goals and believe in yourself. Having a target gets you focused on what you want.

We have been improperly conditioned to think, act and be small. This conditioning comes from your family, friends and society. When you state the big accomplishments you have planned in your life you are beaten back. You are called a braggart, big headed or asked, "How do you think you will be able to do that?"

Why is it ok to be self-deprecating but not have big dreams?

When you say your dreams out loud and talk about achieving them you are positively programming your brain for success. When you verbally self-deprecate you are programming your brain for failure. When you say the words "I am," the words immediately following it go directly into your subconscious mind. So, if you say, "I am a loser," you just added that program. It would be much better to say, "I am destined for great success." This would be a much better program to install. You need to not care about what other people say or think. Don't let them cause you to doubt yourself.

Do not accept false beliefs or the self-limiting conditioning you are subject to.

Notes

What did you learn?

What action steps can you take?

What points do you need to reflect on?

Chapter Eight: Invest in Yourself

When doing a TV interview Warren Buffet was asked "what would be a great investment for the average investor watching the show?". He said, "Invest in yourself. It always gives the best return."

Abraham Lincoln once said, "If I had six hours to chop down a tree, I would spend four of the hours sharpening my axe."

Invest in educational material such as books and audios.

Read books that are uplifting, inspirational and educational. By reading about people's success stories and how they did it, you will see in most cases it did not necessarily come easily but perseverance got them there. This can instill a "If they can do it so can I" mentality. Build belief in yourself. Educate yourself about the law of attraction and how energy works. Read about success principles and things you can do to help move you forward.

Three books I would recommend would be "Ask and It Is Given" by Esther Hicks, "Think and Grow Rich" by Napoleon Hill and "The Magic of Thinking Big" by David Swartz. Saturate your mind with positive information. Don't just read the books, study them and try to apply the concepts in your life.

Listen to audios and keep your mind focused on your success. Like the books you read, they should inspire and educate you. Think about the concepts discussed. Participate in the process of learning and applying. You can listen to audio books, educational audios and even listen to them on You Tube.

Some audios I would recommend would be anything by Esther Hicks or Napoleon Hill as well as "Your Wish is Your Command" by Kevin Trudeau.

When you study and learn you actually grow the gray matter in your brain, which helps develop a younger, stronger brain.

Focus on your personal growth and development. Remember, You Are the Common Denominator in Your Life. Whatever you do to improve yourself will pay dividends in the way of improving every area of your life.

Notes

What did you learn?

What action steps can you take?

What points do you need to reflect on?

Chapter Nine: Mindfulness

Live a *mindful life*. How many people live without paying attention to their lives? They have no focus on what they are doing or where they are going. Things just happen to them. That is because they are driving the car with a blindfold on. It is no wonder that they often get what they don't want in life. They did not participate in consciously choosing what they do want.

Live your life paying attention or being in the moment. When you have practiced living mindfully it is easier to be a more deliberate creator of your life. You can apply this to every concept discussed so far.

Living outside the box means blazing your own trail. You need to be mindfully focused on doing this to be successful. Working with the Universe not against it requires conscious orientation of your thoughts, words and actions toward a positive outcome. Taking personal responsibility is impossible without you being present. Persistence is mindfulness on fire. Aiming high or thinking bigger is a deliberate mindful decision. I am sure the common thread of being mindful and present in the moment is obvious.

Being mindful and in the moment is a mental discipline. There are so many ways to practice and bring it to the point of being a positive, productive habit.

Be focused on what you are doing. Do not multitask since it is the polar-opposite of mindfulness. Concentrate on everything you do. Even keeping your desk or work area clean and neat helps with creating this mindset among other benefits.

Go back to chapter 3 on your thoughts and how important they are. How much of your thinking is on random things, negative experiences, worries and what you don't want? Now contrast that with how many of your thoughts are on your goals, dreams, positive experiences and what you truly want. If you were to keep score between the two on any given day what would the result be? Remember you become what you think about most. Be mindful of your thoughts.

You can do the same exercise with the words you use throughout the day. Using positive, affirmative words has an amazing impact on what happens in your life. There is an equally powerful effect from using negatively charged words but with a not so pleasant result as when you use positive words. The previous sentence is an example of referring to a negative event while using positive words. Be mindful of your words.

It is key to realize the subconscious mind does not hear or recognize words like no, not, don't or any words with a similar meaning. One day I experienced this firsthand and became thoroughly convinced of its soundness. I was speaking with someone who was saying everyone is getting a bad cold lately. Not having had a cold or the flu in years

I said, "I never get sick." Following the above principle, it was no surprise that within five minutes I had a major head cold complete with sneezing, congestion and a headache. I realized what I had set myself up for just after the words were spoken. I am not saying that everything happens that quickly, but my experience did. That is why it made such a profound impact on me. I learned the lesson.

How often do you or someone you are speaking to start a conversation with a negative or complaining statement? Maybe you say how bad the weather is or they complain about the traffic that made them late. This is another great exercise. Just watch this in yourself or those you talk to and see how often it happens.

It has been proven that when you are exercising, practicing yoga or martial arts the results in your body are considerably greater when you are completely focused and mindful of every movement you make. I experienced this in my own martial arts training and witnessed it in the students I trained long before I read the articles written on the subject.

Be mindful with your finances. Are you a spendthrift who wonders where all the money went at the end of the month? If you are being mindful of your spending, you will know where your money went, and you probably planned it in advance. Examine the best use of your financial resources and be fiscally responsible to your budget. How someone spends their money is a personal choice, but the real question is *was it by choice or just mindless actions*? The point is are you present and paying attention?

In relationships and communication, mindfulness is critical. When you are talking to someone are you mindful of his or her reaction to what you are saying? Or are you just talking at them? Their facial expression, body language and verbal responses are all things to pay attention to. If you are truly mindful and tuned in you may even feel their reaction.

In a relationship, whether professional, romantic or otherwise you still need to be mindful. You need to think about how your words, actions or the actions you're not taking make this person feel. One part of being mindful here is to anticipate how they will feel about what you say and do. This way you are deliberately creating the best results possible. Great relationships are built over time and if you are careless and not mindful, they will also deteriorate over time. Be mindful not careless in your thoughts and actions toward others in your life.

Meditation is a great tool to quiet your mind and gain a stronger control over it. Moving meditation is very powerful as well. When doing a moving meditation like Bagua, Tai Chi or Kung Fu forms you need to focus on every aspect of your breathing, the movement and your body alignment. Through this mindful practice you are developing a greater control or discipline of your mind.

Be mindful of all the small things in your life. Remember that small things with time and repetition become big things. This can be applied to positive as well as negative things. Rid yourself of the negative things and build on the positive things.

There is an old American Indian story that illustrates this perfectly. A young warrior was told by the wise tribal elder that in every man there are two wolves. There is a bad (negative) wolf and a good (positive) wolf that fight for control. The young warrior asked: How do you help the good wolf to win? The tribal elder responded: *Just stop feeding the bad wolf and he will starve to death.*

Live your life in a *mindful* way. This will continue to pay large dividends in every area of your life.

Notes

What did you learn?

What action steps can you take?

What points do you need to reflect on?

Chapter Ten: Take Care of Your Health

Let's spend some time comparing the benefits of being healthy to the benefits of poor health. I hope that sounded like a ridiculous statement to you. That being said, why don't people make their health a higher priority? Often it is lack of self-discipline, laziness, bad habits or lack of knowledge on health-related topics. How much time, effort and money do you invest in maintaining your health? Looking at how important good health is, are you doing enough?

A 2015 Center for Disease Control (CDC) report found that over 50% of adults have one or more chronic diseases such as heart disease, diabetes and cancer. 25% of those adults have two or more chronic diseases.

The CDC also reported that two thirds of these diseases can be been prevented with a proper diet and exercise.

Think about this. What is most important? Your good health should be the number one priority. If this is so important why don't more people exercise regularly, make better food choices and look for ways to further enhance their health?

What is more important than the health of your mind and body? If making money is important to you then see how effective you can work if you are sick! One of the biggest reasons people go bankrupt is from piling up large medical expenses. If your relationships are important, well, you don't have much to offer sick in bed. If your children are important to you why not live long enough to enjoy them and possible grandchildren?

I have personally witnessed people who are not willing to commit their time and money to taking care of themselves. Your health needs to be a top priority. Ask someone that is terminally ill how much time, money and effort he or she would give to have their health back. As a young man I had this discussion with my best friend who was 18 years old. His name was Jeff Chapels. Doctors had just amputated his leg and he was dying of bone cancer. He was awarded $1,000,000.00 in a lawsuit and he told me he would have gladly traded it for good health. This was very poignant because it was the same principle our martial arts instructor Grand Master Tom McGee had taught us years earlier in our training.

There are many things you can do to help maintain your good health. I am a strong advocate of martial arts such as Tai Chi, Bagua Zhang, Qi Gong and Body Mind Systems. I favor these because of their focus on building a strong Mind and on Chi development, cultivating and strengthening strong Chi flow through your body means strong health to all your organs and organ systems. Having a well-developed mind is critical to having your mind control your body not the other way around. Your health starts in your mind.

Your thoughts play a big role in your health. Positive thinking causes your brain to release helpful hormones such as dopamine. Negative thinking causes the release of stress hormones weakening the body. Thoughts also can bring up emotions. Qi Gong and Traditional Chinese Medicine teaches your emotions connect to specific organ systems. Emotions such as anger, worry, fear, sadness or grief, often enough can lead to health issues. This comes from the 5 Elements Theory. These concepts are thousands of years old. Science has been catching up and starting to see the correlations.

Outside of martial arts training, I have a fair amount of understanding of many health-related subjects but am not an expert in the field. That is why I am talking about the awareness and importance of taking care of your health as a top priority not a specific protocol.

I would encourage everyone to research and find a form of physical exercise that you can do on a consistent basis. You may want to gather information on foods and the benefits of organic food over GMO foods. Other subjects you may want to explore are vitamins, minerals, supplements and cleanses. You would want to consult a doctor or an expert in these health-related areas. I encourage you to take charge of your health first by educating yourself then by taking the correct action for you.

We can't just go from having bad habits and not exercising to leading a perfect healthy lifestyle. If you can make small changes consistently, over time you will find yourself in a better place.

If You are the Common Denominator in Your Life why wouldn't you do everything possible to be the healthiest you that you can be?

One thing to consider is that the mind and the body are a set that is designed to work in perfect harmony.

Here is a perfect example of just how critical investing in the health of your mind and body is. Your body is like a vehicle and your mind is the driver. If you had one car that had to last you for your entire life how would you treat it? How much time, money and effort would you invest in its maintenance? Would you want to keep all the original parts? In what condition would you want the mind of the driver? I cannot stress the importance of contemplating these questions enough.

One of the first things I was taught in martial arts was that I have one mind and body. There is nothing more important than having a healthy, well-developed mind and body. If your body deteriorates, your mind will follow suit. If your mind deteriorates, your body will too. If you allow this to happen your life will deteriorate as well.

Notes

What did you learn?

What action steps can you take?

What points do you need to reflect on?

In Summary

For some, the information presented here has new concepts to learn and explore. For others these concepts may be familiar. If so, you still benefit. Reading this may give you new insights from the new perspectives.

The understanding that you are in complete control of your life can be very liberating. For some whose lives are not what they want them to be, this idea can be a bitter pill to swallow. It is easier to deny this truth. Better yet, why not make changes in yourself and over time create the changes in your life you want? Taking yourself from where you are to where you want to be is not an overnight process. You need to start, or it will never happen. Making a lot of small changes consistently over time can bring you where you want to go. What are you going to be doing that is more important anyway? Would you rather be the driver or the passenger in your life?

You have a lot of information to process and bring into your life. Do whatever it takes to deliberately create the life you want. It is worth it. You are worth it.

We have discussed ten concepts in Part One. We will be exploring ten additional concepts in Part Two.

Remember you are the central factor in your life.

Part Two

Part Two

Introduction

Chapter One: Gratitude

Chapter Two: Beliefs

Chapter Three: Feeling Good

Chapter Four: Decisions

Chapter Five: Choices

Chapter Six: Either a Gift or a Lesson

Chapter Seven: Who and What Do You Surround Yourself With?

Chapter Eight: Live the Life You Want to Live

Chapter Nine: Work on Yourself

Chapter: Ten: Be a Good Friend to Yourself

Final Words

Introduction

Part Two

You are the most important component in creating the wonderful life you want.

You can view this as a math equation.

You + Your Relationship = A Result

You + Your Job Performance = A Result

You + Your Goals = A Result

What is the common denominator in these equations? You Are!

How do you improve your life? You must improve yourself. Everything in your life starts from within you. Too many people look to the external aspects of their life for their happiness. They may say, "If I had a better job, I would be happy. If I had a great relationship, I would be happy. If I had more money or better health, I would be happy." The list goes on and on. You must feel it from within to experience it in your life. You must feel it before you can have it. It is good to know what you want. The challenge comes when you are focused on the lack of what you want. You must feel it first, and then it comes into your life. You may want to ask, "How can I feel happy if things are not going well in my life?"

We will be exploring the answer to that question throughout this book.

When you are overly familiar with something it is hard to notice it. You are blinded by the familiarity. Using the example of your office there are many small things you don't notice. Now when someone else comes into your office they will notice things you don't see. Some may notice your office is dusty and cluttered. Others may see the office is set up in an inefficient way. They have "fresh eyes" and see things differently. What is closest to you is the hardest to see.

What is closer to you than "*You*"? It may be difficult to truly see yourself. It is sometimes difficult to see our own strengths and our own weak areas. The following chapters will help you to take a fresh look yourself. You will have new concepts or perspectives to view yourself through. Take some time to think about each of them and evaluate if there are changes you can make to improve yourself. You may gain useful new perspectives from this exercise.

You are the common denominator in every area in your life. This means if you improve yourself, by default you positively affect everything in your life. This means better relationships, better career and everything else in your life. It all starts with you.

One thing you can do is read this book over and over internalizing the concepts in it. You become what you think about most. The book was written in a short concise way so you can easily read it multiple times without consuming all your time.

You will notice that the book is not written from conventional thinking. Conventional thinking can often be the reason why you don't have what you want. We will approach things from a point of view using Eastern philosophy, energetic concepts (Law of Attraction), and the use of your mind to construct your life. It is possible to say much of it is common sense. It is worth noting common sense isn't very common. Common sense is only helpful if you follow it.

After each chapter there will be a page for you to write down some notes if you like. You can write what you gained from it, action steps you plan to take or points you would like to reflect on. I know by doing this you will benefit greatly. However, doing this is your choice.

Chapter One: Gratitude

The law of attraction says like attracts like or stated in a different way, what you put out comes back to you. Feelings are the key factor in determining what you are energetically asking for and what you will get. Wouldn't you like to be in a position of having so much to be grateful and thankful for? Here is where it gets hard. You have to be thankful first then you get more things to be grateful for.

You can find anything to be grateful for. You can be grateful for your health, for a nice meal, that it is a warm sunny day, or a cloudy rainy day that is relaxing, or anything you can think of. The point is that you think of it. It can be the smallest reason, but the point is you emit gratitude.

Do not say "I will be grateful when I have this or experience that." That would be doing things in the wrong order. You must be thankful for what you have before you get anything more to be thankful for. You can imagine the experiences you want and feel gratitude for them. Dwell on how good it feels and how lucky you are. This actually speeds up the whole process up.

Start your day with a feeling of gratitude, end your day with gratitude and feel it periodically throughout the day. Make feeling gratitude a habit. Be thankful for everything because you may not know what's there to help you get what you want. Sometimes you need to lose something you have in order to create a void to be filled with something better. A relationship ends only to be followed by a better relationship. You lose your job only to replace it with a better one. Sometimes something happens which looks bad but over a longer period of time turns out to be a blessing and something to be grateful for. It may be a good idea to be thankful for the less obvious gifts. This is why it is important to be grateful for the gifts even when it is difficult to see the immediate benefit of them.

Try and live your life like it is a meditation. Be mindful of what is happening and try to see what you are doing to create it. We are energetically responsible for everything in our lives. Nothing in life is a coincidence or happens for no reason. This is great since it means it is possible to create whatever we want.

I was driving to Whole Foods in Swampscott, Massachusetts and got lost in an audio I was listening to. Not paying attention, I missed my turn to enter the parking lot. When I realized I missed my turn I felt frustration, then my tire immediately hit a pothole. I laughed and said thank you out loud. Who in their right mind hits a pothole in their Mercedes Benz laughs and says thank you? I did, because I could see the law of attraction giving me an instant result. I felt frustration and I got something to frustrate me more. After I laughed and said thank you I saw another entrance. This was a small incident with minimal effect on my life. I thought it was such an incredible learning experience I viewed it as a lesson. Generally the law of attraction has a lag time so you can clearly define what you want with time to adjust it. You wouldn't want every thought or feeling to manifest instantly. This was an example where there was no lag time and the lesson were obvious.

Have you ever sat down and really thought about everything in your life that you can be thankful for? You may look and say things are not so great right now. Be thankful for what you have, it could be much worse.

To put this all into perspective, I had a friend whose pregnant wife missed her train to work and was going to be late for work. This looked like a bad thing right? Her train ran under the World Trade Center and the date was 9/11/2001. Doesn't that change the story? You may have a difficult time seeing the good in something as it occurs but in time it is possible to understand the benefit to you.

Whether something is good or bad is a matter of perspective and time. You can choose your response to events and situations. It is beneficial to find the good in everything you can. You may say, "what if you lose a loved one or someone close to you becomes very ill?" There are many things that can come up in your life that there is no way for you to find anything positive in. I understand that, but what is the benefit of you feeling sad, depressed or angry about it? You will feel bad but then let it go. When things are beyond your control sometimes you have to just surrender to the situation and move forward the best as you can. Try to let it affect you as little as possible by focusing on good things in your life.

Find things in your life to be grateful for and allow more good things to flow to you. Only you have the final say in how you feel.

This can be a form of expectancy. Expectancy is a powerful emotion or attitude for drawing into your life what you want.

Notes

What did you learn?

What action steps can you take?

What points do you need to reflect on?

Chapter Two: Beliefs

There are conscious beliefs and subconscious beliefs. Then there are beliefs that help us and those that hold us back. Conscious beliefs are great because we can see them. This means we can choose not to hold them if they are limiting us and are no longer valid. Beliefs that apply to us when we are young may not apply to us as adults. It is helpful if you evaluate your beliefs throughout life and determine which ones you keep and which ones you discard.

Many of these beliefs came from our family, our experiences and society.

The beliefs that are subconscious are not so easily identified. This means we will have a hard time making changes to them. These beliefs will influence our thoughts, choices and actions throughout our lives. They will do this without our conscious consent. What if you took on the belief as a small child that you were not intelligent or that you were ugly? You don't remember doing that, but you wind up insecure with low self-esteem. What if you took the belief you were poor and the rest of your life you had trouble with making or keeping money?

Your sub-conscious mind has more power than your conscious mind. It is silent and invisible but works at directing you 24 hours a day. How can you win a fight with the invisible man?

The brain is like a computer. You program the computer, which runs you. Everything you see, hear, think, believe, experience and say is stored in the programs in your computer (brain).

I would highly recommend that you read the book "The New Psycho-Cybernetics" by Dr. Maxwell Maltz. It explores this concept in-depth and is an amazing book.

Many of the beliefs we hold are false. Unfortunately, our brains do not know that. Your brain and sub-conscious mind takes in everything you feed it as fact and responds accordingly. Your subconscious mind does not judge what you're telling it. Give it thoughts and beliefs that help you. Tell it what you want not what you don't want.

What if you fail on a real-estate deal and you take from that the belief that you can't be successful in real estate? I have heard several serious real-estate investors say, "If you haven't had any failures in this business, you haven't even entered the game yet." If you go with a belief based upon one failure, you will have deprived yourself of one of the greatest investment vehicles out there. This is the point. Our subconscious beliefs can hurt our future when they are not real, and they get in the way of our success.

Now for the good news... you can rid yourself of these unwanted sub-conscious beliefs. Not only that but you can program the beliefs you want to have. Programming your brain isn't difficult, you just need to be aware of what you are feeding it.

I told a story earlier in the book, which is so relevant here I will tell it again.

There is an old American Indian story that illustrates this perfectly. A young warrior was told by the wise tribal elder that "in every man there are two wolves. There is a bad (negative) wolf and a good (positive) wolf that fight for control of him." The young warrior asked, "how do you help the good wolf to win?" The tribal elder responded, "*just stop feeding the bad wolf and he will starve to death.*"

Try and feed your mind as much good information as you can. Make it a choice and then make it a habit.

Getting rid of the bad programs is a little more difficult. You can address it with energetic methods. I have used many modalities for clearing these issues. A few that I found effective are:

Body Mind Systems

Meditation

Practicing Qi Gong (Chi Gong), Tai Chi and Bagua Zhang

Thought Field Therapy or more commonly called TFT with Joanne Callahan.

QEC Quantum Energetic Clearing with Lee Beymer

I-Ching Systems with Mary Miller

Best Technique - Morter Health Systems

We choose our beliefs knowingly or unknowingly. Our brain and sub-conscious mind take in everything around us. Being aware of this we can be in more control of what information is being put into our brains and sub-conscious minds. We use this information to form our beliefs.

Notes

What did you learn?

What action steps can you take?

What points do you need to reflect on?

Chapter Three: Feeling Good

You may have learned from Esther Hicks that we must be feeling good in order to manifest positive things in our lives. If you are unfamiliar with this concept, I would strongly recommend you read the book or listen to the audio "Ask and It Is Given" By Jerry and Esther Hicks.

What does that really mean?

Well if you understand that your emotions have a dramatic effect on what you draw into your life it means a lot.

What happens in your life is largely affected by the feelings you are putting out. Thoughts mixed with emotions are emitted from our brains and we receive back the same frequency in the form of our reality. So, having positive emotions is better for us.

This doesn't mean that you are flying high every minute of every day. It means that you strive to be in a positive state more than in a negative one.

Emotional responses become habits too. Choose these habits with care. This may be difficult but is worth the effort.

What if you say, " I don't buy into the law of attraction, positive thinking, energy and all that quantum physics stuff. So how is this going to affect my life?"

Who would you rather be married to, a person with a positive outlook or someone who is negative?

Would you want employees who have positive attitudes and emotions or the opposite? Who would you rather have serving your customers and representing your business?

Who would you like to be in these examples?

How you are feeling affects those around you and how they will treat you.

Therefore, it is important to be feeling as good as you can as often as you can. It has a big effect on your life and makes it much more enjoyable.

It is to your advantage to make an effort to stay in a more positive emotional state, feeling as good as possible. Do this even if you feel like you are faking it at first. You are trying to gain positive momentum and form new habits.

This is not a new or novel concept but how many people use it to their advantage?

Think about how you react to things emotionally. What are your conditioned responses? Are they helpful or harmful to you?

Notes

What did you learn?

What action steps can you take?

What points do you need to reflect on?

Chapter Four: Decisions

What truly is a decision? Well, let's look at where the word came from. The Latin roots *de* and *caedo* mean literally to prune or cut off and the Latin verb *decido* came to mean to decide. When you prune a tree-branch, that branch is gone. When you make a decision, you remove all other options and go in one direction only. So, it is safe to say that a decision is a choice that is backed by full faith in its attainment and total conviction. There is no doubt. Failure is not an option here. Failure isn't even a thought in your mind.

This reminds me of a story of how a general won a battle he had little chance of winning. His army sailed to do battle with an army considerably bigger than his. After taking the army to shore he instructed his men to look back at the ships. They looked and saw the ships in flames. They were told they would win or die, there was no retreat. I call that having to make a decision. In the Art of War this is called death ground because you have victory or death. There are no other options. You still have to decide on victory.

I have had many personal experiences in which I made a decision. I had a complete feeling of knowing the outcome I wanted was going to happen. Keep in mind that anyone else looking at the situation would have thought I was completely delusional. In other words, achieving my goal did not look possible. However, I would literally feel it in my gut and knew I would succeed. I did not just believe it, I knew it. On these occasions the only thing that could derail my plan was doubt, which is a poison to success.

I believe a true decision is an energetic event. You can feel it in every cell of your body. It is a feeling of complete certainty. You feel it is already done; you are just waiting for it to physically appear. Everything happens in the mind first, then it becomes your reality.

If you look back over your life you may recall times in which experiences that have brought you great accomplishments. They were most likely the result of a decision. Making a decision is a very empowering experience. When you want something, first make a decision to have it. Know there is a difference between making a decision and wishing for something. A decision is a commitment to success whereas a wish is not. You will be better off if you make more decisions in your life.

Notes

What did you learn?

What action steps can you take?

What points do you need to reflect on?

Chapter Five: Choices

Throughout this book, I go in depth into the concept of taking responsibility for everything in your life. One area that people often neglect to understand is that everything we say or do is a choice. Do not confuse a choice with a decision. A Choice precedes a decision. Every choice you make gives you a result. Every result comes from choices you made. Whenever someone says, "I had to do it" or "They made me do that," they are wrong. They made a choice to do it. When someone says, "I have to go to work" that's not true. They choose to go to work because if they didn't, they would most likely get fired. You choose to eat because you would starve if you didn't, plus you enjoy food. Yes, these examples are simple choices you easily make every day, but they are still choices. Choices are made based on outcomes and consequences.

Some choices are more difficult than others. Choosing one job over another, choosing a spouse or where you live are big life choices.

If you say, "I can't afford that," technically that isn't always accurate. You have chosen to spend your money on something else that has a higher priority.

There are day-to-day, perhaps minor choices that can also be challenging, but these choices go a long way toward creating your circumstances. For example, someone says something to you that you disagree with. You let it go, or you argue your perspective. Is it worth souring a relationship over? This is a choice. When something happens that you don't like, you choose your emotional response as well as your reaction. Consider this example: You are driving to work and encounter heavy traffic, which makes you late. You have two choices at that point in time. Option one would be to become angry and blame the traffic for making you late. The other option is to accept your situation and take responsibility for it. You can say to yourself, "I should have planned better and left for work earlier. Next time I will." There is no benefit to choosing option one, which only results in raised blood pressure and increased stress. You start your day feeling miserable and this can follow you throughout your day. Choosing option two, you are empowered because you took charge of the situation and accepted responsibility for it. Either way you are late but how you feel is your choice.

These choices can feel just as difficult as the big life choices you make. It is helpful to consider that all the small things can add up to big things over time.

So how does this concept help you?

Too often people make choices conforming to what society dictates or to please others. Your first responsibility is to yourself. Considering others in making a choice may be appropriate but not if it is harmful to you. When you do something that isn't good for you to please others, it is always a bad choice. For example, when you were a kid and the other kids were smoking cigarettes and put peer pressure on you to do the same. You always have a choice to please others or do what you feel is appropriate. There are many societal pressures that people feel *they must yield to*. When you do anything only because it is what others *think you should do*, that is the wrong choice. It is good to consider how your choices affect others, but ultimately you must consider your own happiness.

If you choose a career because it is what your parents want for you even though it is not what brings you happiness and fulfillment,
what kind of life is that?

Happiness comes from within. If you are not happy within, no external thing or person can make you happy. Everything starts with you. Whenever you do anything it is a choice. Be mindful and choose wisely. Your choices can form patterns, which define you. You are the common denominator in your life.

Notes

What did you learn?

What action steps can you take?

What points do you need to reflect on?

Chapter Six: Either a Gift or a Lesson

I touched on this subject earlier in the book. It is a topic important enough to discuss in more depth. Earlier I stated that there is a saying I coined which is, "everything is either a gift or a lesson. In actuality they are all gifts, although some hurt too much to feel like they are gifts, so we call them lessons. In the end they are all gifts, bringing us what we want or something we need to learn."

Life teaches us the lessons we need to learn. We only learn these lessons if we pay attention and are open to learning them. Then we need to take corrective action. The lesson can come to us in a subtle way. If we don't catch a lesson the first time, don't worry. Life will keep turning the volume up until we figure it out. It is still up to us to learn the lesson and make the appropriate changes.

It is important to take a wide view of the situation and time. I explained in the first chapter on gratitude that things often happen in your life that appear to be bad. It may have been a necessary event to bring what you wanted. Let's say you are clear on what you want. Then things happen that appear to be disasters. It is so important to understand that sometimes the sequence of events necessary to achieve your goal can be and sometimes must be a rocky road. After reaching your goal and looking back at the road it is obvious why things had to go the way they did. But it can be very challenging to understand at the beginning before everything has unfolded.

We have probably all experienced this at some point in our lives.

I know this first-hand. Years ago, I was facing a situation that looked like it was going to be a disaster to me. This was the type of situation to which a normal response would have been fear, worry and sleepless nights. Instead I was totally confident things could work themselves out. Then I had several dreams in which I was told everything would work out perfectly and there was nothing to worry about. Subconsciously, I knew everything would be fine. It is important to understand that there was nothing I could physically do to help my situation. It wasn't even my situation but the results of it would have major impact on my life. The only tool I had available was my mind. I kept in my mind, thoughts of everything working out perfectly. The situation continued to look hopeless as time passed, then at the very last minute it was resolved in a way that was better than I could ever have imagined. The sequence of events changed many things in my life all for the better. It truly was a gift though it didn't look that way for several months. In the end it was unequivocally a blessing and a gift.

Look for the gifts and lessons in your life. Remember gifts don't always look like gifts and lessons need to be learned.

Notes

What did you learn?

What action steps can you take?

What points do you need to reflect on?

Chapter Seven: Who and What Do You Surround Yourself With

Have you ever considered how the people in your life and your environment affect your life?

Let's start with your family. What kind of family did you grow up in? Were your parents' positive, supportive and always encouraging you to succeed? Did they teach you to believe in yourself by believing in you first? Or were they pessimistic, focused on the lack of money with a "We can never get ahead" attitude? Either way, this was imprinted on you and your beliefs. If you grow up poor it is common to have a poverty mentality. It could be all you know. It can also produce the opposite effect causing you to reject poverty as your future. You may develop a burning fire within you to succeed and be willing to do what it takes to live a different life than the one you were exposed to. If education is stressed in the family, you may see that as something important and pursue a higher level of education. If it wasn't, you may not see education as being important. The people closest to you often influence your beliefs, the choices you make and the direction of your life. You can't choose your family but you can choose what you accept or reject from your experiences with them.

If you grew up in a loving and nurturing environment or were surrounded by domestic violence this will influence you. However, you still have the ultimate choice on what that effect will be. Children often grow up adopting the views, beliefs and habits of their parents. As an adult you do have complete freedom of choosing for yourself. So, you have the ability to reject or retain this powerful influence. It is truly a choice.

You can look at a plant. If the plant is grown in good soil it has an advantage. If the plant grows in poor soil it has a disadvantage. Nevertheless, adversity can be turned into an advantage with persistence. Have you ever seen the plant that grows and pushes through concrete sidewalks or parking lots? It finds a crack and perseveres and flourishes. Conquering the adversities in your life can help you to become someone you could never have been without them. I can honestly say I am thankful for the adversities I have experienced in my life. It has forged me into the person I am today.

Look at who you associate with or your close friends. There is a saying that *birds of a feather flock together*. You can take it a step further and say you become who you surround yourself with. If you associate with people who live a very healthy lifestyle, chances are you will be influenced to live that way too. If you associate with heavy drinkers of alcohol you may find yourself drinking more alcohol. Most people don't like to stand out due to fear of criticism, so they conform to their environment. This includes doing what those around them are doing.

If you surround yourself with people whom you would like to emulate you have a tremendous advantage. There is so much to gain from this.

Spend time with people who have or are what you want to have or be. What are the advantages from these associations? First, they are an example that it can be done. This helps cultivate an "If they can do it so can I" attitude. Next, you also see what and how they think through their views and the attitudes they live by. Do they confront a situation that looks bad and look for a way to make it work to their advantage? You also see how they live, their habits and actions. Did you know that successful people vacation more often than unsuccessful people? This is not just because they have more money to do so. It is actually part of why they became successful. There is a lot to this point. A few of the reasons are when you take time to recharge your battery, you are feeling good which attracts good things into your life. When you relax, you free your mind to have greater vision and enhance your ability to create. You also strengthen your immune system, so you are healthier. By witnessing all of this first-hand you see which thoughts, habits and activities will bring you closer to what you want.

Now what if you surround yourself closely with people who are living a life that is not the life you want? It is similar to what would happen if you surrounded yourself with people who have the life you want. The only difference is you get what you don't want. The process is the same, but the outcome is different.

As a teenager, I began associating with nine fellow students who were training with me to become martial arts instructors. We spent most of our time training and socializing with each other. The result was that six of us went on to become martial arts masters, a high rate of success in this field. Our association with each other gave us a great advantage in our pursuits.

One thing that holds us stuck in a pattern of disadvantageous behavior is *emotional agreements*. This is the glue that binds us to the behaviors of our surroundings. So, what is an emotional agreement? The people around you come to expect you to think and act in a way that they are used to. You tend to comply and stay the same. It maybe you fear criticism, drawing attention to yourself or you just fear change. Remember when you do grow and change, the others become different compared to you and now they stand out. This can make them feel susceptible to the criticism you were afraid of.

A simple example would be: If you have dressed the same way for years, the people around you expect a certain look from you. You want to change and dress nicer, but it feels funny and everyone comments on it. Even positive change can feel uncomfortable.

Another example would be when you make a decision to improve your health. You adopt a healthy lifestyle, exercise daily and focus on improving yourself. Those around you don't want you to change this way because that forces a change on them from what they are used to. They want you to remain the same, fulfilling an unspoken emotional agreement about who you are in relation to them.

Changing belief systems can be especially hard.

Plus, breaking or changing emotional agreements can be awkward and uncomfortable.

You can slowly but deliberately evolve the change over time. The alternative is to make a clean break. Sometimes you receive a gift in the form of change thrust upon you through events in your life. An example would be when you want to start living a healthier lifestyle, but it conflicts with the lifestyle you're used to and share with your friends. Then you have a mild heart attack and the change becomes easier to make.

This could be considered a form of momentum, which was discussed at length in Part One of this book.

Your physical environment is very important. If you work or live in a stressful environment it can have a negative effect. Living or working in a positive and fulfilling environment can produce a better result. When you live or work in a cluttered workspace there is an energetic issue to contend with. This is where Feng Shui principles can be of help to you. One of the concepts used in the practice of Feng Shui is enhancing the energy in a space and its free flow. You don't need to be an expert in the field to be able to make helpful changes to your physical surroundings. You could hire a private Feng Shui consultant or just read up on the subject. Even small changes can have a big effect.

Here are a couple of examples of how I have used Feng Shui principles with great results.

I was struggling with a relationship situation. While reading about Feng Shui I realized I had a pet Piranha in the relationship corner of my home. I thought having a predator and a goldfish killing field in my relationship corner was not doing me any favors. So, I decided to move the tank. I made some changes and focused on what I wanted. Within two weeks I had completely changed my situation.

Many years ago, I was facing a big business challenge and didn't see how to fix it. I did two things. I continued to study Feng Shui principles and brought in a Feng Shui consultant. Following the information I learned and the advice of the consultant, I made changes to my business environment. I went from facing my worst year to having my best year. Yes, my thoughts and faith that I would overcome my situation certainly played a role. Although the fact that I was taking inspired action toward it was paramount in the process. It backed my thoughts and faith with an action step to help me focus on achieving the outcome I wanted. Changing the energy in my environment gave me a significant advantage.

Take a look at who you surround yourself with. Then look at your environment. What do you see? What changes can you make?

Notes

What did you learn?

What action steps can you take?

What points do you need to reflect on?

Chapter Eight: Live the Life You Want to Live

In order to be truly happy you need to live the life you want to live. We have touched on this topic throughout this book. There are so many choices to make that define the life you are living. The choices you make need to come from your heart. You should never give in to pressure from others when you are determining the life you want.

There are many aspects that comprise our lives. What career path do you want? Do you plan on getting married and at what stage of your life will that happen? Do you want children? Where do you want to live? You may have family members who would like to help you answer those questions. Society has set its definition of how we are supposed to go through life as well.

Why not dare to follow your dreams, passions and do what would bring you the happiness you want? You are the one living your life. Don't you think you should be the one making the decisions?

Notes

What did you learn?

What action steps can you take?

What points do you need to reflect on?

Chapter Nine: Work on yourself

What this all comes down to is developing yourself to your full potential. This can mean working on yourself mentally, physically and energetically.

Having good health is a priority. It is important to develop the external body but developing the internal body is where your health is truly affected. Having strong organ systems is key. You need to have a strong, unobstructed chi flow throughout your body. I highly recommend martial arts training. The martial arts I find the best for cultivating and promoting strong chi flow would be Tai Chi, Bagua Zhang, Chi Gong and Kung Fu. Personally, I train in Body Mind Systems, which includes training in all of the styles listed.

Along with a strong, healthy body you need a strong, healthy mind. Training the mind through challenging, rigorous exercise builds will power. This translates into mental toughness. Having strong will power enables us to deal with the challenges we encounter throughout our lives. This allows us to stay on track in living our lives and achieving our goals. We all will have challenges that we need to overcome. Will power leads to persistence, which is a key to success.

Through mindful training, you develop mindfulness. I dedicated an entire chapter to mindfulness in the earlier in the book. It is a very important quality to develop.

Program your brain and sub-conscious mind. Your brain and sub conscious mind are being programmed throughout your day by the media, music, what you read, and anything and everything you are exposed to. It is like a sponge absorbing all the information around you. Even your thoughts and words program your brain and sub-conscious mind. It is possible to consciously program your own brain and sub-conscious mind. Do the best you can to limit your exposure to negative information like the news, music with negative lyrics and most advertisement. You then will want to expose yourself to positive, uplifting and inspiring information.

Learn new skills or information. Learning keeps the brain younger and healthier. The process of learning actually generates new brain cells.

Work on communication and social skills. Improving these skills will give you an advantage in life.

Ultimately, it is about continuing to grow and improve in any way you can. The more you improve, the more you have to offer yourself and others.

Notes
What did you learn?

What action steps can you take?

What points do you need to reflect on?

Chapter Ten: Be a Good Friend to Yourself

Be good friend to yourself. What does this mean? It means treat yourself like you are the most important person in the world and it's your responsibility to care for you.

Note that the better you treat yourself the better you treat others. One of the first big realizations I had from training in martial arts was the more you respect yourself the more you respect others.

How do you talk to yourself?

Your thoughts and internal dialog has an effect on you, as do the words you say out loud to yourself and others. This was discussed earlier in the book when we talked about programming yourself. When you criticize yourself, you are harming yourself because you are putting a negative judgment into your subconscious mind, which it accepts as a fact.

Any time you do anything to yourself that is harmful in any way you are not being a good friend to yourself. Here is a litmus test. Take something you say or do to yourself and ask yourself one question. If someone else said this to you or did it to you would you consider them a friend or foe?
Why not say empowering and encouraging things to yourself? See yourself as a success and a great person. You choose what you think and say to yourself. With this power why would anyone want to choose to say negative, discouraging things to themselves?

I have encountered people who literally hate themselves and self-sabotage their lives. They are their own worst enemy. It comes down to the fact that they have a horrible self-image. This leads to self-destruction and unhappiness.

Your self-image is developed over time. It is created by both what you think of yourself and the opinions of others that you accept as true. This is why you need to have the best possible opinion of yourself. It is also important to reject unfavorable views of others. You have the final say in determining your self-image. Be a good friend to yourself and give yourself the greatest self-image possible. I am not saying to be full of yourself and look down at others as inferior. I am saying to believe in yourself, care deeply about yourself and do whatever you can to be helpful to yourself.

When you eat healthier foods, exercise your body and focus on continuously expanding as a person, you are being a good friend to yourself.

Notes

What did you learn?

What action steps can you take?

What points do you need to reflect on?

Final Words

What happens when you are driving and drift into the lane next to you and someone honks their horn? They are informing you that you're off course. Life or the universe does the same thing by giving you what you need to see to stay on a productive course. Sometimes it whispers and other times it yells. If you live mindfully, you can maximize this assistance. Your world is a reflection of you. If you want to know what is going on inside, you look at what is going on around you. If you don't like what you see, improve yourself and your surroundings will improve.

Everything is energy. Energy is always in motion. You are energy, so you are always moving even if only at a sub-atomic level. You are either growing or dying. That is why this book is focused on your growth.

I hope you gained some valuable insights from reading this book. Some points discussed within the book may have been reminders and others may have given you new perspectives. Both are valuable and helpful.

About the Author

 My name is John Calabrese and I am originally from Chicago, Illinois. Currently, I am living on the North Shore of Boston, Massachusetts.

Professionally, I am a Master Level teacher in martial arts, speaker, author, and entrepreneur. With over 30 years of teaching experience, I have expanded into the speaking and literary fields.

Learning and teaching are my passions. It is my belief that learning is to accumulate knowledge but to teach and apply knowledge is to transform it into wisdom.

In 2002, several other Master Level martial arts teachers and I formed Body Mind Systems, a martial arts organization and system.

Body Mind Systems training is focused on the complete development of a student and their ability to apply the training and principles in their daily life.

Learning about and training in the use of the mind and energy in martial arts led me to expand my pursuit of knowledge to learning more about the Law of Resonance (Law of Attraction), natural laws, success principles and their application in life.

I feel blessed to have written this book and to have the opportunity to share this information with you. It is my hope that you enjoyed and benefited from its concepts and perspectives.

John@growthisadecision.com

Visit www.Growthisadecision.com

www.ingramcontent.com/pod-product-compliance
Lightning Source LLC
Chambersburg PA
CBHW072039110526
44592CB00012B/1477